She Would Draw Flowers

Kirsten Savitri Bergh

A Book of Poems

First Printing April, 1997
Second Printing May, 1997
Printed by Sentinel Printing, St. Cloud, MN

Photo credits:
Opposite preface by an anonymous friend, 1996
Kirsten & Nina on page 86 by Marianne Dietzel, 1996
Back cover by Molly O'Brien, 1996

Table of Contents

In Memoriam
Kirsten Savitri Bergh
July 7, 1979 - November 29, 1996

Preface

Against the general pessimism about today's adolescents, this small volume flings out lines of joyous poetry like shafts of sunlight across leaden skies.

These are young poems that depend more on the intensity of sudden awakenings, to new perceptions of the world and of an emerging self; depend more on an enthusiasm that sweeps the lines along; than on patient, mature polishing and the building up of logical structures.

Kirsten's natural directness and sincerity satisfy us deeply. She seeks not only heights but depths, in poetry that illuminates and is illuminated by the mysteries of life, love and death. The poems to her father are remarkable and subtle instances of this.

She discovers analogies and interrelationships within the cosmic and the earthly and a breathing that unites the self with the world. Her awareness of such living realities, even though youthful and dreamy, is in itself the very medicine and healing for the dis-eases attacking us today.

Kirsten's mother has worked over the arrangement of these poems, keeping in general the sequence in which they were written and incorporating newly discovered poems in the most appropriate places. Then she has fitted Kirsten's pen-and-ink sketches to the form and mood of the printed pages. The result for us is a fresh breath of joy, a sense of the unfailing sun that flames and glows in the book's last poem.

– Christy Barnes
Harlemville, NY

A letter from Kirsten to Nina the day before they died.

To Nina, my love,   *Nov. 28, 1996*

Listening to "Two of Us" (Beatles), joy fills me, shimmers through me, knowing that although we've made so many thousands of sunny or cloudy memories together, "the road that stretches out ahead" will be so much longer–so many adventures and loves and laughter and tears and sorrow–just so much life lies before us, the "two of us".

[Imagine] how we will grow strong and beautiful (even more than we are now!) and become grannies together: rosy, apple-cheeked, cloudy-haired grandmothers who will tell stories to the grand-babies about iced-grapefruit chapstick and moose and about our childhood loves and losses, about the hours and days spent together, the years, the centuries; two girls becoming women. And then we'll cackle at each other with twinkling eyes and laugh till we cry. Then when they all go to sleep, or go away, we'll slip on our Converse and go dancing the night away under the moonlight.

But that is many years, many miles away. Our feet will dance over so much earth, our ears hear so much music, our hands touch so many people, our hearts love so much! I'll see you golden and glowing with babies and me, too, perhaps. The world will be a little bit better because of us, even if our names are forgotten after our death.

But death won't stop us, it's only another lake to swim, another slight climb before the next mountain peak. But 'til then, 'til tomorrow, I'll remember to love the snow and you'll begin to love skirts over sorrels and the world and life will hold us like a mother.

Happy life, dear sister.

Introduction

Kirsten Bergh and Nina Dietzel died suddenly in an auto accident on November 29, 1996. On the day before they died, Kirsten wrote the note on the facing page to Nina. It was written on a card that she had originally purchased for Nina's birthday but must have misplaced in her room. I imagine she found the card while cleaning her room in preparation for my arrival on Thanksgiving and was inspired to write this spontaneous message.

Kirsten was seventeen when she and her friend Nina died. I had come to visit them in Harlemville, NY where they were both attending Hawthorne Valley, a kindergarden through senior high Waldorf school. I was a passenger in the car with them and was the sole survivor of the accident. My last memory was feeling our car slide out of control as we rounded a curve into the path of an oncoming sixteen-wheeler. It was later reported that black-ice conditions were the probable cause of the accident.

Kirsten left a legacy of paintings, drawings and poetry which she wrote during her high school years. These are among the few tangibles I now hold to remember my daughter. But the profound path of her inner transformation shared in these poems has also served as my guide for letting her go. As I share them with others, I discover that they, too, find a pathway to her. This pathway, in spite of all the pain of loss, remains open.

So, I offer with this book a means by which all who knew and loved Kirsten might rekindle feelings of warmth, love and compassion for her. I believe that these feelings of warmth will find their way to her as nourishment and help on her continuing path. As a mother, each day facing this unimaginable loss, I question how I might remain connected to my beloved daughter while leaving her free to journey on.

I find answers in the poems that Kirsten has left. It is my hope that you will also experience the comfort, inspiration and hope that these poems continue to awaken in me.

– Linda Bergh
April 5, 1997

1

Part One

This section of poetry shows Kirsten's living connection to nature and her feeling of belonging in the world. At this time, she had not been touched by any personal loss or tragedy. She attended kindergarten through eighth grade at the Minnesota Waldorf School located in the Minneapolis/St. Paul area. Her Waldorf education was rich in oral tradition and the arts which developed her sensitivity to the living beauty of nature.

This early training and attitude was not lost on Kirsten. It was strengthened by our family's passion for nature, literature, the arts and our spiritual work. Her gifts were first evidenced in her very descriptive writing in the elementary grades. From fourth grade:

"Winter is the time of year when crimson streaks the horizon and sparkles on the newly laid snow. It's like an angel slipping around the world scattering love all over."

From a seventh grade poem:

I wish I was an eagle with a hooked beak of gold
Ebony wings that have seen things, seen tales untold
Wings that have carried me high above care
High above worries that vanish in air
High above treetops blossoming green
High above oceans speckled with frills
High above green and sheep dotted hills
High above meadows by babbling brooks
High above sparrows being pestered by rooks.

But not all of the pictures I've seen have been sweet
I've seen lonely vultures hungering for meat.
A bloody plain with men in pain,
And brothers fighting brothers, toward what aim?
There are men of peace and men of war.
Some of whom care none for the others.
I wish as an eagle
Flying high above,
That every being on this planet
Could someday know love.
Could someday know joy and harmony and peace
I wish as an eagle that our fighting will cease.

Before Kirsten's freshman year in high school, we lived and worked in France for a year while she attended a Waldorf school. She became enveloped in French literature and poetry which she reveled in reciting. When we returned to our home in Minneapolis, which we were sharing with the O'Brien family, an English teacher from her public school inspired the muse in Kirsten to re-awaken. She began to carry an "idea book" to capture words as they came.

The following poems were born.

PURPLE VIOLETS

My path has never been strewn
With broken glass
And cutting words.
No,
I have walked my life
With feet pale and tender,
On pillows of purple violets,
Embraced by yellow voices
That enfold me,
Leading me, with trusting eyes closed,
Away from the sharp, slippery rocks,
Away from the sucking pool
Which threatens to pull me under,
Shielding me with gentle blue-sky wings
From the screaming, tearing, empty wind
Which tries to blow me away.

I did not ask for this path,
For the loving smiles
And guiding hands,
But they are mine.
This is how I am.
This is my path.
It is mine to walk,
To change as I please,
To take care of
Forever.
I must cherish my violets,
Or they will die.
So I will,
Forever.

FOOTPRINTS

We strolled along the beach together,
The ocean and I.
She fingered the shiny pebbles
That I let drop.
She filled my wandering footprints
With her own watery feet,
Leaving subtle valleys,
Glazed with silver
On the sand.

We played tag,
The ocean and I.
She burbled when she caught me,
Tickling my toes
With tentative fingers.
She reached into her
Deep shadowy pockets
And tossed out creamy shells
Onto the sand
For me to gather.

We spoke of many things,
The ocean and I.
She whispered to me
Tales of faraway lands,
With castles high on hilltops green;
Of crystal beaches
And golden suns.

I talked to her of sneakers,
And of marbles,
And of how pretty a daisy looks
When it dances in the wind.
When we tired of talking,
I collapsed on the sand,
And listened to the ocean
Sing me her lullaby.

And when evening descended,
We watched the sun go down
Together, the ocean and I.

CRACK OF DAWN

Dawn breaks: an egg.
Its golden yolk oozing
Through dusty shutters
Making a sticky
Puddle of warmth
On blue tile floors.

Frying and sizzling
In its own heat
On a frying pan
Of black asphalt
Parking lots.

A trickle of morning
Seeping through
Cracked church doors
Staining much-trod aisles
And worn wooden pews
Yellow with its touch.

Trickling through
Trees, black branches
Haloed by fluttering leaves
To spatter sidewalks
With sleepy images
Of tiny dancing suns.

ODE TO RINGO

From the back comes
The heartbeat of a star
A timeless rhythm
A persistent voice
Building pillars
For the winds to wind about

Behind the snares
Looming large in his legend
His grapefruit grin
Spreads like a rumor,
A contagious malady.
An eternal catalyst,
It blends with his beat
Gathering worshipers
For him to shine upon.

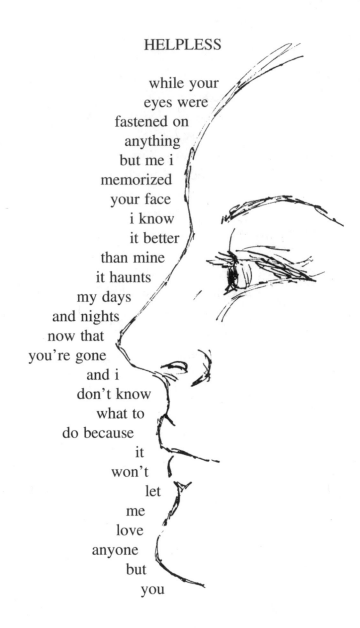

HELPLESS

while your
eyes were
fastened on
anything
but me i
memorized
your face
i know
it better
than mine
it haunts
my days
and nights
now that
you're gone
and i
don't know
what to
do because
it
won't
let
me
love
anyone
but
you

AYLA

She stood,
Pale hair blowing
In the young wind,
Pale eyes searching
The young world
For a trace of herself.

Seeing hands touched the wind
Knowing feet kissed the earth
Pensive smile tasted the sun,
Asking for her way.

LA MARGUERITE
Comme la lune
Qui chantait
Des étoiles
Elle m' a dit
Avec un soupir
Qu' elle voulait être
Une marguerite
Qui danse
Dans le vent
Alors je l'ai pris
Par la main
Et je l'ai enseignee
A danser.

THE DAISY
Like the moon
Who sang
Of the stars
She told me
With a sigh
That she
Wanted to be
A daisy
Who dances
In the wind
So I took her
By the hand
And I taught her
To dance.

13

THE SANDBOX KING

The King of the Sandbox,
His dimpled cheeks ruddy,
A scratch on his elbow,
His overalls muddy.

A ruler who reigns
With a firm yet fair hand
O'er his people of stones
And his kingdom of sand.

As he gallops away
On his hobbyhorse steed,
To rescue fair damsels
And aid those in need.

A red plastic shovel
Is held at his side,
To serve him as saber,
His weapon, his pride.

Each army he battles
Is quickly cut down
By the King of the Sandbox
Defending his crown.

His regal gold crown,
Which so proudly is worn,
Is a newspaper hat,
Now soggy and torn.

His hands are all grubby
From ruling the land,
And his once-proper shoes
Have filled up with sand.

A smudgeon of dirt
Has appeared on his nose,
He has scratches and scrapes
From his head to his toes;

But the King of the Sandbox,
His shovel in hand,
Continues to rule
O'er his kingdom of sand.

SHADOWS

Shadows play
Like music
In the
Wrinkles of
Her face. She
Knows all
But doesn't
Always understand
Why.
She is like a
Tree being
Blown by
The wind
Only because
It knows no
Better. She
Will not
Search
For a new
Way, she
Does not
Need one.
All she must
Do is nod
Her head,
And smile.

17

ODE TO YOU

You are a dancer:
Lithe, like the wind;
Beautiful in movement
And in form.
You are an actress:
Enthusiastic, passionate
You embrace every role
With sensitivity and love.
You are an artist, a writer:
You create vibrant worlds;
Pictures and words
Flow like water
From your fingertips.
You are a musician:
You fill your world
With resonant melodies,
Somber and sweet.

You are all of these things,
And many more,
And you are my sister,
We will always be sisters,
Not of the blood,
But of the heart and soul,
Which are perhaps stronger bonds.
We have gone through many changes,
And will go through many more together,
But they will never
Change our love because
We belong together.
Though we follow
Different paths,
They will never
Tear us apart because
We are a part
Of each others lives and destinies.

So do not despair,
My lovely Ophelia.
Though we may separate,
As all souls must do,
We will always
Come back to each other
Because
We are sisters,
And we love each other.

ODE TO MY TREE

We have grown together,
You and I...

Even now, as I sit, cradled
In your leafy embrace,
Gazing through your speckled leaves,
I feel no difference between
Today and yesterday.
Your strong branches have always
Supported me,
Held me,
Caught me when I slipped.
Your dancing leaves have always
Created a canopied chamber
Where I can hide.
When the wind swayed your branches,
I clung to you, feeling your breath.
When I come home,
Your feathered arms greet me,
Beckoning,
And I answer your call.
No one else responds.
Only I have explored your kingdom,
Stood balancing on one bare foot,
Trying to move with your rhythm.
Although others have climbed
The flimsy ladder into your arms,
They grew tired of your silence,
Of your stillness.
But we are alike, you and I.
We have changed together,
Adapted to each other.
Now, as your newborn leaves
Flicker and flash in the sun,
I can see your smile.

We share a secret,
You and I.

STORM THOUGHTS

All of a sudden,
Everything, the air, the trees, the sky, the people:
They are all darkened by the storm.
The tree outside my window one moment ago was still,
Now it thrashes in the wind, a chaotic, wild dance;
Now it's obscured by the rain pelting the glass
Of my kitchen window.
Headlights shine like frightened eyes,
Followed by shadowed bodies.
The storm is destructive, tearing, but also healing.
It seems to seduce me, drawing me into its fury.
Outside I stand hesitant, protected from the rain,
But still my bare legs are the victims of the stinging spray.
The wind whips away my breath, emptying my lungs of air.
Forcing me into the storm.
Its power, its angry roar, they invade my chest, fill me.
It rules me, and everything else.
It shows no mercy, no pity, yet means no harm, I think.
The sky flashes, growling, roaring,
Threatening my haven of safety.
Making my heart tremble.
The radio sings in the corner, unaware.
How long will it last?
The storm will eventually destroy it,
Destroy us all.
Its tears stream down my window,
Seeping through the cracks,
Invading me.
Black birds still fly outside,
Can't they hear the voice of the storm?
Don't they fear it?
Perhaps they know it better,
Perhaps they're not as näive as I.

Already my tree is calmed,
Though the rain still drums on the glass.
The sky still rumbles, more like drums than the rain.
The wind doesn't torment me now.
I can hear the splashes of the cars in the streets,
They're all less cautious now.
The sky is lighter now, the rain not so violent.
Now it's gone altogether.
The radio is still there.
So am I. I think.

OPEN YOUR EYES

Open your eyes!
Can you not see the pale green leaves,
That cling, like a gentle mist,
To the black branches of the trees?
Will you not smile at the purple violets
Who nod cheerfully as you pass?
Do they not bring you happiness?
The creamy blossoms dancing, floating
Like fragrant snowflakes on the breeze,
Do they not fill your heart with gladness?
Look! Can you not see the sunlight,
Shimmering and flashing on the water?
The blue sky fluffed with lazy clouds?
Can you not see their joy?
Can you not share it?
The air is filled with song:
The wind whispers in the trees,
Blackbirds warble out their melodies,
The water chuckles happily to itself,
Distant thunder grumbles harmlessly.
Will you shut your ears to their gentle voices?
Will you shut your eyes to their compassionate smiles?
Do not close your heart to the joy and beauty around you,
Rather, embrace it.
For if you cannot love the world, you cannot love yourself.
And without love,
There is nothing.

TO A SMALL BOY SEEN IN THE PARK TODAY

Listen, small boy, to what I have to say.
I can see, by the light in your smile,
And the innocent glee in your eyes,
That you have forgotten
That your striped shorts
Are faded and torn,
Your blue shirt
Dirty and old.
You have forgotten
The dirt under your fingernails,
And that your feet
Are scratched and brown
From always being bare.
I see that you
Have laid down
All of your loads,
Light or heavy as they may be,
To chase after
(your brown feet flashing over the emerald grass)
A straying wisp of happiness,
A white fluff, floating
On the warm breezes
A wish, a dream,
Or perhaps all it gave you
Was a moment of pure pleasure,
For when you captured it,
Held it cupped in your
Brown, careful hands–
A delicate trophy:
One to be treasured,
And then set free;

You smiled at me
As you ran past,
And your smile told me
What your foreign tongue could not.
I saw the purest happiness
In that brief glance,
The joy that only children,
With their hearts open,
Can experience.

May all of your dreams
Be as simple to capture,
And give you as much pleasure,
As a fluff of dandelion seed,
Floating on a sunbeam,
Has given you today.

DRAGON TEARS

I can see my heartbeat
In my eyes, it is pale
Like the sky
I can feel it in my fingers
And even in my chest
And still the clouds
Build their cities
Large enough
For a child's smile to hide in.
But thoughts escape
Through yellow walls
Even if they're lined with thunder
They flee through marshes
On a lullaby of windy sighs.
Whispers, like drips of laughter,
Of a fountain dragon's tears
Trickle across the sun
And kiss it like an eyelash
Ever-so-softly touching a cheek.
I can see my heartbeat
In my eyes, but that is all.

Part Two

When she was 16, Kirsten's father, Paul, died suddenly from a cardiac arrest. Her view of the world and herself changed dramatically. Kirsten was not able to say good-bye to someone who was so close to her that he was part of her every breath. Although we often shared our grief with one another, Kirsten's most important healing came through her journaling and poetry. In August, 1995, nine days after Paul died, Kirsten wrote:

"I can't imagine life without him. I know he'll still be with us in spirit, but I want, I need, his body, his brilliant mind, his loving heart. I miss his horrendous habits that drove me crazy. I'll miss the man, the daddy, the person I knew for 16 years."

And one month later:

"My life is a confused heap of memories and dreams. Sometimes I wish I could've remained back there–back then. But I have to move on. I will be happy no matter what happens. My tears of grief will mix with those of joy."

Shortly after her father's death, Fred Destailleur, a friend from France, came to stay at the Bergh/O'Brien household for a year. During this time, Kirsten, as a young woman, was full of the struggles and joys of adolescence including romances, friendships, losses and changes.

Her poetry of this period demonstrates her authenticity, directness and her will to move through pain to transformation. The last three poems in this section reflect her stretching to a very deep place to find her center. Through poetry, Kirsten was able to grapple with grief and find peace and joy.

TEARS

Tears were
entangled
in her eyelashes;
looking through them
she saw a blurred
world, lined with
rainbows
where laughter
never ended
and memories
didn't make you cry,
because
nothing that was good
ever went away
for long.
And hearts were
pumped
with love
and never failed
because there
was
always enough
to go around.
And death
was only a relative term
instead of an end.
The tears swelled
and slipped,
silent
as her sigh,
down her cheeks,
leaving only
their pale traces,
and a futile wish
behind them.

MAYBE

Maybe now that my life has crashed
and lies around me in shattered pieces;
maybe now that my hopes for tomorrow
have flown off like night moths;
maybe now that the sweet perfume
from the flowers of my dreams and wishes has faded,
and the petals begin to drop off;
maybe now that the darkness of my fears
has almost suffocated me;
maybe now that my heart wishes to be broken
to get it over with;
maybe now that I am stripped of everything
but my naked soul;
maybe now, you will let me love you.

JUST PAUL & ME

And then it's just
Me and Paul
And the night.
Him just crooning
About playgrounds
And women
And nonsense
With a scratchy
Old record sound.
And me just
Twirling
With my reflection
Like some
Fancy-dancy
Make-believe queen
Dancing the polka
And the night
Just sitting there,
Staring at us
As if we were
Crazy,
Or something.
I guess we are,
Because I'm all alone,
Just me
And my reflection.
Put that in one of
Your songs, Paul:
A crazy girl
Dancing with her
Shadow
Because there's
No one else left
For her
To dance with.

SUN PATCHES

Sun patches on my knee
and I want to drive forever,
or 'til the mountains ripple
in the air
and the red shoe-coating dust
swirls around you
like smoke when you stomp
and shuffle and twirl
in a breathless dance
and the earth, all
red and orange and brown
moves and sways

and then it's only me,
lying on my belly
under the sky
and my fingers
drawing circles
in the hot silk dust
with a small, white rock
looking me in the eye.

LIKE THE DAWN

How can I think
With these voices
Filling up every crack.
I know and love
The sound of
My other language.
If it came rolling out,
Soft and deep and throaty,
At best,
From another pair of lips,
Lips like mine, or so they say–
Maybe I could hear the music.
But not tonight.
I can almost grasp it–
The smile in the voice,
But now it's gone.
And the world is blurry again,
Or until there is an extra
Water spot on my page.
Because although I
Can feel his laughter
In my yellow desk-mate
(A porcelain hog sporting a
purple waistcoat)
And his face grins a
Silly smile from my wall:
Un nouveau papa,
Eyes planted on my
Baby face,
He left me alone.
And he forgot to even
Say good-bye.

Now all is silent,
Though the cars
Whisper by through the night.
And I'm afraid of my heart,
And my mind, which
Paints me with memories.
And my body becomes
A twisted rock,
Streaked with rain.

Yet though it seems
Like another day would hurt too bad,
Another word would cut too deep,
My yellow companion
Smiles at me from behind
His porcelain pipe,
And I know that my smile
Will return,
Like the dawn.

TO MOLLY

Oh darling,
He wasn't worth the sunlight
That plays in your hair.
His smile not as bright,
Nor his embraces as warm.
You may wash your pillow,
And my arms,
With the hot tears
That streak your fevered cheeks,
But do not let your heart,
Which you let him steal,
Be thrown away,
Or shattered.
For you will love again,
You will be enchanted
By another pair of dancing eyes
And honey lips,
And yours will cry again.

You were my flower,
My little tree whose
Gentle beauty and grace
I envied.
But now,
As you wrap your
Trembling branches around me,
As sobs wrack your slender trunk,
As you come to me for comfort
In your pain,
I see.
I see your envy of me
In your brimming eyes,
I hear it in your moans.
I have what you have not.
I am ignorant of this pain.

He turns away,
Holding your heart in his hands,
Knowing yet unconscious
Of the pain he causes
With just one glance.
You smile and bend
When he is near,
Trying to keep from dying
Because his smile,
The one you love,
No longer belongs to you.

FOR A LONG TIME

For a long time
she kept her heart
sealed in a tall
blue bottle.
It
must have held alcohol
or something,
because when she finally freed her heart
it was drunk
with joy
and made
her feel giddy
with laughter and love.

A LONG WAY

You know,
we really have come
a long way.
I mean,
we've learned
how to make
lime jello,
and scented candles
and how to tie our own shoelaces.
That's actually quite
a large step
when you think about it.

MOTHER

The sun filters through the ripples of white swirly lace.
Dapples, yellow, a paper valentine heart
of shadows and sunlight on the countertop.
A soft image, of sunlight, of yellow warmth, of lace hearts.
Contentment, peace.
Your arms surround me,
enfold me in yellow warmth,
shining loving light into my heart from yours;
a lacey heart, beating with your strength and love.
In your softness I find my contentment and peace
You rock me, cradle me with your assurance,
Your knowing of me, your selflessness.
Hold me in your soft embrace a while longer,
I will spread my wings and take flight soon enough.
And when I do, my heart will always cherish
the comfort and love that I find only in you.

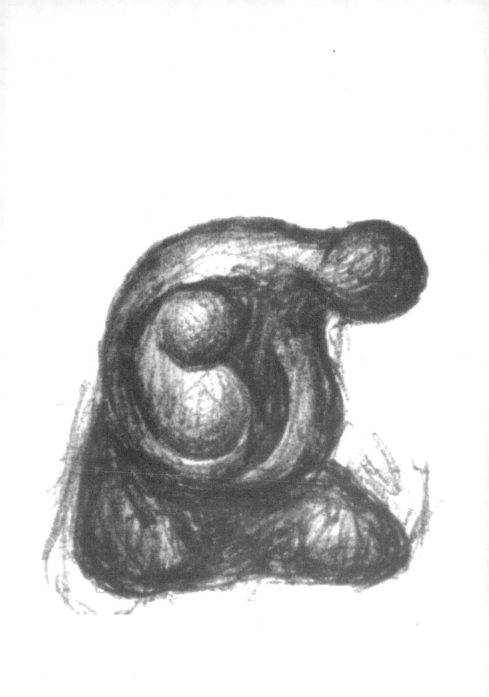

MY KING

And you shall be my king
she said, and placed a
crown of dandelions
on
his head and kissed him
on the nose.
And he smiled
and laced his
slender fingers with hers
and they ran laughing
through their kingdom.

SUNSET PAINTER

Well, I guess you know
how to paint sunsets now
Just like you always wanted
Maybe
They made you
Chief Sunset Painter
and you make the clouds a
just-so-salmon and
are the expert at blending
peaches and blues
And you paint every evening
Even the cloudy ones
And there are no more
restrictions
Because the sky has no limits

FOR YOU, PAPA

I thought I heard your footsteps
running toward me,
disturbing the stones.
But when I opened my eyes,
I saw it was only the waves,
pulling and swirling like hands.

I thought I felt your smile,
Warm and loving upon my face.
But when I opened my eyes,
I saw it was only the sun,
Beaming at me from across the water.

I thought I heard you
Whisper my name.
But when I opened my eyes,
I realized it was only the wind
Playing in my hair.

I thought I felt you
softly kiss my cheek.
But when I opened my eyes,
I saw it was only a leaf
Caressing me with gentle strokes.

And then I felt your love
In and all around me.
Powerful yet gentle like the waves,
Warm and shining like the sun,
Soft yet strong like the wind,
Tender and alive like the leaves.
And I didn't even have
To open my eyes.
I knew you were there.

SANDALWOOD

As the grey loon light of your death day dawns again
I hold you in my palms.
You seem vulnerable, but as all dust
You are impenetrable,
Out of danger for the rest of eternity.
You float on rose petals
Until the water claims you as its own,
And you disappear, misting gold in the clear water.
But that is not you,
Those ashes tossed to the wind.
That is just your crumbled shell,
Nothing more.
Where is your smile, your rolling laugh,
Your warm sandalwood hugs that kept me safe
From the winds of the world?
Now only my hands lie between you
And those same winds.
But now I've let you go
And I'm alone with my tears
And a memory of warm sandalwood in my heart.

REMAINS OF THE STORM

That night
when the frogs chuckled
in the darkness
and the lightning bugs got tangled up in the vast
web of stars,
the trees dripped the remains of the storm.

THE NIGHT

She trailed moonlight and fireflies
behind her like perfume, and her
velvety cloak of shadows slid like a
sleepy sigh across the hills.

WOODWORK

After she left
This emptiness
Devoured him
But he soon began
To notice
Her face,
Smiling down at him
From the curls in the woodwork.
Her laugh,
Rolling soft
In the rhythms of the rain.
And he felt
Her kiss,
In every falling snowflake
That caressed his cheek
And slid down his face
Like a forgotten tear.

SHE WOULD DRAW FLOWERS

She would draw flowers
(yes, her mark, but not
enough like a swastika to make
them look twice)
wherever she felt an
empty place
(which was everywhere).
So they filled up the walls
and cluttered up the corners, and
dripped onto the floor in a
rainbow puddle,
which the people
(yes, smooth-brained wrinkles
with starched shirts)
slipped in.
And they squeaked at her to
scribble on paper
(yes, their telephone-wire paper) if
she had to make a mess.

But she could only hear
the colors of her flowers,
and they filled up her mind
and her body
until her skin (thin like a petal)
could take no more
and fell away.
And she became a rainbow.
And her colors shone their music.

And the people
(yes, colorless and bagged like bread)
forgot to wear their
overshoes
when they walked in her puddles.
So bit by bit, they
soaked up
her scribbles
(instead of slipping)
and bit by bit,

They each became a flower.

NEW GRASS

Sweet,
close to my face
your breath is like new grass
the kind that pushes green
cradles the brown mustache of winter
until it fades.
Did you kiss me then?
Two sunspots your eyes,
like the ones that
danced in the trees.
Your arms held me like a baby
and the grass cradled us
pushed green against our backs
until we faded
like the old,
and disappeared.

MAYBE MY HEART

Maybe my heart will be washed
away like dust in the rain
that shakes the trees and cries like
ghosts outside the walls that shiver
and sigh in the hands of the wind
and I could see you as just a stone
in the river of my life, as just a
beautiful boy with a tender heart
and not the subject of the ache
that throbs at night and the image
that haunts my dreams

UP HERE

From up here
you are all very little
Not less important
Just easier to deal with,
and harder to love,
like strangers.

Up here I am queen of myself,
and follow no one's rule
but my own.
I am the chosen
The Maker-of-Decisions
I decide when to laugh
And when to frown;
What to think
And what to love.

Up here, I piss where I want to piss.

I am untouched by rejection
Anger and Fear
By all save
The sun, the rain, the wind
And the rocks beneath my feet.

And up here, I am always beautiful
Always free

And up here,
I am always alone.

READING YOU

I would like to scream
like a siren at you
But I won't, 'cause
I know what you
would do. See, I can
read you like a book,
sometimes. Yeah, and we
got the same battle
tactics, the same escape
plans. So I might as
well scream at me.
Sometimes I forget to
read between your lines,
and I lose my place,
though I try to
remember to fold down
the corners when I stop
reading. And sometimes
you're just you and
there's no me reflecting.
And that's when I gotta
get out my dictionary.

ROCKS

his words fell
like rocks from his mouth
and clattered all around him.
even after
the avalanche had cleared,
I could feel them jostling
around
in my head
keeping me awake.

CORNER DRUGSTORE

I remember a long ago time
when I would collect
postcards like this
where you couldn't
tell the difference
between the real
and the reflection.
The water was so still
and the trees
were silhouetted
like a city against
a loon-call sunset.
Now I go looking for
my perfect postcard
place, instead of buying it in a corner
drugstore.

..TWO
COWBOYS

KIRSTEN '96

AS BROTHER & SISTER

As brother and sister
or maybe just friends now.
Just like it was always supposed to be
Now that you love me again,
And know that I've always loved you,
We can live together without fear or shame
And forget to be angry.
And I can pretend that
you're not leaving tomorrow,
That my life isn't changing
As swiftly as the weather,
And kiss you on the cheek.
And remember today as beautiful
since that's really all that's left us.

SYMPHONY

Well, your time with us has ended,
with a last breathless shudder
of tympani and tambourine
like the final releasing breath
of a passionate song.
But looking back
across the runs of staccato ups and downs
and the days of soft legato
our year together looks more like
a whole album
with the greatest hits on the cover.
Symphonies braiding,
gentle minuets that flowed easily
with our sincere laughter and love,
harsh banging and cracks of a modern mood;
the blues rolling deep and melancholic
followed by joyous tremolos of soprano and flute,
the notes soaring high
on silver wings of friendship again.
Daring and young
the guitars of our humor roared rock and roll
never missing a beat
whirling rhythms of drums
confused and frantic as our hearts
and sweet voices
humming love songs and lullabies.

The record has ended now
but more will surely follow.
Thank you for dancing with us
through all the music.
The house grows silent.

LINDSEY

I could forget
And hold you forever,
Cradle your dear head on my shoulder,
Your hair shining toffee in the sun,
And lose myself in your smile.
I could forget,
And we could be princesses together
And run hand in hand
Under an African sun
Our laughter eternally young and joyous.
I could forget
And we could become women together
And learn from each other
The secrets of love and pain.
I could forget
And you might never know the difference.
But I can't.
For my heart beats
To a different rhythm now
And my soul cries out for more.
To kiss your cheek,
And promise you forever,
That my darling I cannot do,
But our hearts are linked
By more than dandelion chains,
And our rivers flow
In much the same direction.
And may join again.
And when they do,
We will braid flowers in our hair,
And dance barefoot,
And remember. . .
And our love will be
Stronger than before
For we will have grown wiser

And more beautiful.
And we will know each other
From the laughter in our voices
And the tenderness in our embraces.
Of all this I am certain.
So though I cannot ignore
The beckons that pull me
From your arms,
And must follow my river
That parts from yours
I will remember,
And love you,
Forever.

EARTHQUAKES
(for Mara)

At night I cry
Moon tears streak my cheeks
I think of you
And of my life.
Only the sunny pictures remain.
And my body
Ripples with sobs.
Like a gentle earthquake.
The earthquake
that is splitting me
In two.

REASONS WHY PEOPLE ARE LIKE BUBBLES

-all different sizes but all are basically the same
-all filled with rainbows
-all reflect their environments
-some go up in pairs, some stay single
-all begin at the same place
-all go different places
-most float up as high as possible for them
-some hit bottom
-some last longer than others
-some won't pop when touched; some will
-all pop eventually
-all end up at the same level

MANNEQUIN MOON

Sometimes the moon gets lost
In the city, among the globes
Glowing fluorescent
Strung like onions
Along the spines of the bridges;
Among the drooping streetlights
Hanging heavy with light;
Behind the square office eyes,
The pale boxy teeth, grinning like
An unfinished scrabble game;
On the looming black blocks of buildings,
Posed like dominoes.
But you might find it
Gleaming from an upstairs window
Like a light left on;
Glowing like mercury
In a shadowed-alley puddle,
Or peeping like a frightened face
Pale and timid,
From behind the sharp crack
Of a blackened corner wall;
Or maybe shining double
Like car headlights
In the useless glasses
Of a mannequin in a
Glass shop window,
Rounded and white
Like polished pebbles.

ELDERS

now we are the elders
'round the fire
looming tall in the shadows
not yet as wise
as the pines
but wiser than before
for we have spoken
with the mountains of yesterday
bathed in the streams of tomorrow
and lain in the flowers of today

RAIN BIT

The rain bit bullet holes
in the thick gray dust
as we trudged road-weary and chatty as ever

(Mere) MIRROR IMAGE

Who are you, girl, who always meets my gaze without hesitancy? You, who smiles when I do, who mimics my every motion as if you could read the thoughts that pass through my body and brain.

But you, my imitator, whose actions show what I feel, you, gazing back at me with a face that everyone, even I, have been taught to recognize as myself; do you feel what I feel? Or does the glass allow only the reflection of my skin to pass through to you?

If we met on the street, would we recognize ourselves, and embrace like long lost sisters, or pass by, careful not to touch as strangers do? Would we admire each other's tastes and looks and be best friends? Or would we see the hidden nastiness and turn away in annoyance and disgust? If we met on the street, who would be the imitator then? Would we both break free from our bondage?

Each day, after we routinely check on each other's state of being, do you, too, walk out your door and face a world of challenges and conflicts and love? Do you learn the lessons that I learn on your own? When we look at each other through the glass again, do you understand my anger or fear or love or do you laugh inside yourself at my slow progress?

Do you wonder who I am as I wonder who you are?

Am I your reflection?

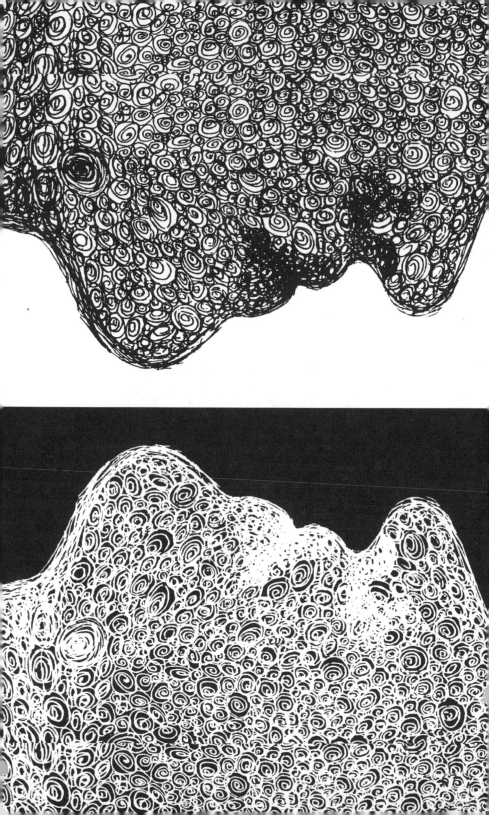

GIRL ON A ROCK

She sat on her rock
like a queen on her throne
just like a girl on a rock
but it was her throne.
In fact, there she would sit,
day after day, watching the sky turn
from gray to pink to blue,
watching the clouds chase
each other across the sky.
Watching the sea beneath her feet
swell and breathe and
turn rainbow with the sunset.
She would rescue drowning
insects with her toe and
dry them with her breath.
And once in awhile
she would pull up her skirt
and slip one foot, and then the other
into the water, and step
gingerly to the shore.
There she would tend her fire.
When she had made sure that it was
crackling happy again
she would return to her
stone, and resume her
watching and sitting.
She never used her fire,
just tended it.
And sat,
and watched.
And that was all.

And then, one evening
as the water
rolled in ripples of gold
and silver,
as the sun sank slowly
into the sea,
all was calm.
She removed her clothes
and slipped silently
from her rock
into the water
leaving just the tiniest
of ripples behind her.

With no one to tend it
her fire went out
and her throne
sat empty.

But occasionally
a passing wave
would gently set
a struggling insect
on a rock,
and a warm breeze
would blow it dry,
with a hint of
a smile on its
windy lips.

BEGINNING BAREFOOT

Why bother writing a poem for which no words come? If I could be the tree's interpreter or translate the language of spiders, maybe then I would have something valid to tell you.

Perhaps if I sit here long enough, watching the shadows jump and swirl on the pine needles, listening to the laughing of the water on the stones, the scratching of a hidden beastie in the dead leaves, feeling the tickle of spider toes on my knee, smelling the bitter mouldy breath of the lichen; I will begin to understand.

But comprehension doesn't come with the wind at its back. So I sit here, all hunched up in restricting jeans, and shoes, and useless clothes which I wear to protect myself from my own society, too restricted by my thoughts to let go of myself and sink into a pine needle and feel what it feels, to slip inside a spider's skin and scuttle into crevices in the bark.

Why can't I stick my toe into the silver water and let my body dissolve into ripples of cloud reflections, feel the fishes darting through my liquid skin? Why can't I stretch like the trees until my skin cracks like theirs and my fingers explode into bursts of green leaf joy? Perhaps I could if I stayed long enough to feel their delight and their anguish, to watch and listen and learn how they are, to understand where this joy that swells up through them 'til they can hold it no longer comes from.

And when I find the source and drink from it, I will understand. But until then, until I have learned to become silent and simple and humble and wise enough to be accepted in the forest and to be shown all its secrets, I will watch and listen and learn. . .

And begin by going barefoot.

70

A LAKE OF MIRRORS

This is a lake of mirrors.
Look deep enough into its clear waters,
Past your own gaze
Past your own smile,
Look until the face gazing back at you
Becomes but another passing reflection
Of the outside world.
Look until the two eyes
Fixed on your own
Become but two pebbles at the bottom;
Your smile but another ripple.
And when you have lost
The face you know so well,
When it has become
just another part
Of this lake of mirrors
When you find that
You can no longer find yourself
Or what you once considered yourself
Look still further.
Look until the pebbles
Mix with the sand,
With the weeds
And everything becomes just color.
No real shapes or forms–
Not things anymore
Just color.
Look until all the colors blend
And become just one color.
A nameless colorless color.
And when you have found this,
And in doing so–
Lost all that you thought you knew before,
Look just a little bit deeper.
All will become clear

Like a limitless mirror
And there you will find a soul.
Perhaps it is the soul of the lake
Or perhaps you will find that it is your soul
Or perhaps they are one and the same.
Perhaps we are all
Just a lake of mirrors
Hiding a soul deep within.

Part Three

In the summer of 1996, Kirsten and her closest friends, Molly O'Brien and Nina Dietzel, were the youngest attendees at a Waldorf conference for persons 18-25. The purpose of the conference was to continue and expand upon the spiritual, artistic and nature curriculum for young adults. They came home with a new understanding of Waldorf education and anthroposophical life. Kirsten & Nina wanted to finish their education at a Waldorf high school. This wish resulted in their move to a beautiful area in rural New York where they attended Hawthorne Valley Waldorf School. They boarded with a family, walked down the road to school and thrived more than we as parents could have ever imagined.

Cecilia Elinson, the mother of Kirsten's new friend Zusha, writes of this period:

"Kirsten lived in Harlemville for three months. Time can pass, barely mixing with our blood, leaving us uninvolved. Or, time can be so rich and deep that our lives are transformed, even in a few short weeks. The latter was the case for Kirsten.

"In Harlemville, Kirsten was surrounded by a warmth that flooded towards her. She breathed deeply of this sun-like force. And she breathed out love for all, without reservation. Age was no barrier.

"Embracing her friends continually, Kirsten was un-abashedly joyful. Lifting many of us off our feet on a daily basis, she placed us down on a new piece of ground and changed our hearts forever.

"Kirsten was passionate in her striving to understand the essence of each individual. Her thinking was strong and clear. Her yearning was to overcome boundaries and find connection."

The poems in this last chapter of her short life are filled with joy, friendship and reflective intuition.

SCARF OF DREAMS

That night
when the stars fell
streaking diamonds
high above the pink
city-night haze,
I sat in my room
and knitted my scarf
of dreams come true.
The colors shone bright
and warm and
only a few stray strings
disrupted the pattern.
With every row I wove
I binded myself to another someplace
far away from the
city's purr and
the backyard crickets.

Now there will be
other crickets and
different night noises.
The stars will be clearer,
the moon brighter,
but not more beautiful.
And the never silent
silence of the city will wait for me,
the back yard crickets will
sing softly in the
shadows of the
streetlights,
until I return.

THE SUN IS SHINING

The sun is shining
the sky is blue
Shall we go out
in the world today
The air is sweet
The day is new
Adventure is only
a footstep away
There are drums to be played
There are bells to be rung
There are thousands of
Heart-lifting songs to be sung
Shall we ring them?
Shall we sing them?
To the beat of the drum?

TO ZUSHA

Forgive me
if I accidently
slip and fall
into the rainbowed
pools of
your eyes
they are lined
with crystals
and reflect the forest
floor

...like incense in a fire
you burned unnoticed
your spirit curling sweet
and mysterious
hiding in their smoke and
ashes

...Oh but I love you 'cause
you make my body want
to dance and I'm on fire
filled with your
cinnamon music

77

MAYBE

Maybe I've
loved you
since
before the
mountains
were hills
and ached
for the sky
and
we
can remember
what it's like
to be green and
rolling
and
fall in love
again and
again

ASK

Would you come
if I asked
and hold my hand
and walk with me,
barefoot,
over long, wet meadow grass
under the moon?

Would you lie close to me
if I asked
and keep me warm
in your arms
and laugh with me
under the starlight?

Would you tell me
if I asked
of the dreams of your heart
and trust me with your tears,
as we walk through the woods
under the rain?

Would you sing with me
in harmony,
if I asked,
and dream with me
of castles and somedays,
as we sit and swing
like children
under the haloing branches
of the trees?

Would you dance with me
in the sunlight
and kiss me without shame
and smile at me with your eyes?

Would you love me
simply and openly
like a flower
if I were to ask?

And would you anyway
even if I didn't?

ACROSS TO YOU

my thoughts roll over each other like
notes in a song
tumbling and tossing like pebbles in a
stream that giggles and twists
like the wind dancing in
the meadow grass running
skipping jumping twirling
like a flaming leaf
caught in an updraft
spinning along the ground kissing
the late summer flowers
rolling through the sky like a
feather
floating gliding soft
as a whisper
touched by tenderness
drifting settling comforting
across time and space
to you.

LOS OJOS DE LA NOCHE

La noche cae
Las colinas están negras
Y el cielo está semejante a un arcoiris
En el que la luna blanca nada.
Yo, sentada debajo las estrellas en el frio.
Pienso en mi vida y del futuro
Las estrellas son los ojos de la noche
y ven todo . . .
Pero me siento que estoy ciega

THE EYES OF THE NIGHT

The night falls
The hills are black
And the sky resembles a rainbow
In which the white moon swims.
I, sitting under the stars in the cold,
Think about my life and of the future.
The stars are the eyes of the night
And they see all . . .
But I feel that I am blind.

(translated by David Gallardo)

STARRY WATERS

That night there were supposed to be meteor
showers, but even though we watched 'til
our butts hurt from the rocks and our
breath formed hoods around our heads, we (I)
only saw three. They must've all fallen
into the lake though, because I could see
them down there, glimmering like eyes in
the blackness.

AUTUMN QUEEN

She walked through the sun trees and blessed them with
her smile and they in return covered her with their
honeyed leaves, which she wore like a cloak of
feathers through the long months of darkness
and where she went she left in her wake
warmed hearts and dreams of autumn days.

LIKE SPECKS IN THE LIGHT

We drift in and out in the spotlights like dust
finding recognition and short-lived fame in sun shafts,
floating on the winds of life,
shining and smiling like a star,
among other stars
blinded by the light of fame until the winds shift
and we're back in the shadows again,
anonymous
though no different from any other lost dust speck
searching for the light.

TO NINA & ME

When we're grandmas together
Maybe we'll be soft and beautiful like clouds
And sweet and rosy with laughter like apples
And we'll be free and graceful
Like the summer grasses
Of our barefoot youth.
Maybe you'll still have dimples,
Curled up like two fetuses in your cheeks
Creased with countless births and smiles.
And maybe there will still be
Freckles scattered across my nose
Like the huts of an African village in the heat
Hiding in the wrinkles that gather at my eyes
Like animals 'round the water hole.

And we'll tell our wide-eyed grandbabies
About iced-grapefruit chapstick.

LAST ENTRY IN HER JOURNAL

I walk
with my breath
up our road
of everyday,
new in its Thanksgiving gauze of snow.
The trees like princesses
getting dressed
in their first layer
of silk and lace.
Some already with pearls
embroidered close enough
to their skin
so that it shone out
almost black
in the fading blue light
almost too elegant and
lovely to be
the same trees
in November peasant rags
as were there yesterday.

PAPA

Did I swallow your spirit
When my mouth was open and dry
From the wails of despair that shook my body?

Did it slip through your soft dying fingers
That I held like cool shells
In my own hands, not daring to let go,
And mix with my blood?

Did it seep into my every pore
Like your living odor, when I held you
In my arms and listened to your fading heartbeat?
Was it in the air I desperately breathed
When I sang all our old songs to you
Until my body tingled and collapsed?

Did it fill me like a dream, like a new love,
Like a baby that is the new me, the you-me,
Who laughs and dances and embraces living?
Are you the stream of joy in my thoughts?
The laugh tickling my throat, the
Lightness in my heels?

So, I carry you in me,
not as the fading memory of a father,
but rather as a growing, glowing child,
until we become one,
and I can let you go.

Did I swallow your spirit
when my mouth was open and
dry from the wails of despair
that shook my body? Did it slip
through your soft dying fingers
that I held like cool shells
in my own hands, not daring to
let go, and mix with my blood?
Did it seep into my every pore
like your living odor when I

held you in my arms and
listened to your fading heartbeat
Was it in the air I desperately
breathed when I sang all our
old songs to you until my
body tingled and collapsed?
Did it fill me like a dream,
like a new love, like a baby
that is the new me, the you
me, who laughs and dances
and embraces living. Are you the
stream of joy in my thoughts?
The laugh tickling my throat,
the lightness in my heels?
    So I carry you in me, not
as the fading memory of a
father, but rather as a ghostly
child, until we become
one, and I can let you go.

glow'n?

SUN

Of course they worshipped you
You are the god of the sky.
You sequin each morning's frost and dew
And paint the leaves and pebbles golden
In the evening.
You are the greatest artist of them all.
Your sun-shimmers are far more beautiful
Than Monet's, even in his prime,
Your skies more vibrant than Van Gogh's,
Your sunsets far lovelier than any
Romantic painter in his most inspired moment.
It is towards you that the plants reach
In their seasonal song of green and gold.
It is a longing for you
That makes the moths dance around flames
And makes the people build their night fires
On the cold hills.
No sweet curve of the moon,
No sloping line of hills,
No graceful arch of birch
No child's smile
Would be seen without your light.
You bring us rainbows
And mornings
And warmth
And life
You give without receiving
And always will.
Above all else,
You
Deserve to be worshipped
And so, great artist,
We will return your limitless love
With our own,
And smile our light upon you.